Chaos Within

A collection of poetry and prose.

ISABELLE RUBY

Ruby Inked Pages

Print ISBN: *978-1-7642574-0-4*
EBook ISBN: 978-1-7642574-1-1

Table of Contents

***For every woman**
who wakes each day carrying battles no one sees.
For the ones who have been lost inside the roles they were
told to play, who have quieted their own names in the noise
of survival.
For the women who ache to be known, to be heard, to be
seen—even by themselves.
Chaos Within is for your healing as much as it is for mine.
May you find pieces of yourself in these pages, and may
they remind you that you were never truly lost.*

Her Tapestry

Her life was a delicate tapestry interlaced with harrowing stories of abuse, pain, loneliness, and suffering. But wreathed amongst those fibres were wrinkles of hope and strength. It was amongst those colourful threads of survival where she rebuilt herself, one stitch at a time.

These are her stories…

Poet of the Moon

The moon, a luminous pearl. Its silver strands of light weaving through the darkness, painting whispers of magic, ethereal promises.

My silent guardian, watching from the heavens as it stirs my soul; sacred and ancient stories, words creating medicine, love, guided by the healing and tranquil light.

A nocturnal haze, an enchanting spell, ever a celestial beacon, forever whole. My timeless muse, my eternal dream.

Our Souls

In the depth of our souls, where mysteries reside,
His essence and mine intertwine.
Across the vast expanse of eternity's flame,
Our love burns eternal,
Forever the same.

Women of Roses

Women and roses are one of the same; nurtured by the same sun, born of the same soil, and picked for our delicate beauty.

Like the rose, women are too often only chosen for their beauty—not the care required to nurture them, nor the strength within to grow in even the harshest of conditions.

Too often, men are mistaking our thorns for mere decorations rather than the stinging shield of protection we grow out of necessity, to protect the tenderness within from a world intent on confusing love with possession, and admiration with entitlement.

Nonetheless, we continue to bloom. We emerge from the soil, time and again, our beauty renewed, our spirits unbroken.

Every thorn a reminder we are not to be handled carelessly, that beneath our soft beauty lies a strength born from survival—a resilience that no man, no matter how careless, can ever truly destroy.

Home

There were moments he was the sun, warming my entire
being, selflessly, lovingly.
Other times, he was the rain; cold, and unwelcoming.
Still, his heart was my home, and home was what I craved.

Empathic Poet

Dear Mama,
I hope you are proud of me.
I've taken the pain of growing up without your presence
and turned it into empathy.

Dear Dad,
I hope you are proud of me.
I've taken what I survived in silence
and turned it into poetry.

The Kind of Beautiful

He was the kind of beautiful that was hard to love; he drank too much, and he broke her trust. Too often, he left her shattered on the floor, picking up her own broken pieces. He took her for granted and he knew it. He promised to be better, relying on her rose-coloured hope in him to blur reality.

She was the kind of beautiful that was simply too pure for this world.

Scarce Love

She needed love

But not from just anyone

She needed love from the people she loved

For someone to look at her and see her light

Her kindness

And her worth

She needed them to see her pain

To hold her heart

And heal her soul

That unconditional type of love

She needed a parent's love

The unwavering, no-strings-attached kind

The kind that seemed so rare and increasingly scarce in today's world

Love that every child deserves

But evidently not every parent can provide

Their Blessing

All she wanted was for everyone she loved
to look at him and see everything magical
she saw in him.

Orphan

I was young when I learned the way things worked; how people chose favourites, how love could be rationed, and others were constantly prioritised above me. I was just me. Always too much or never quite enough. Too sensitive. Too outspoken. Always one step too wrong in any direction. I could never get it right. Too often I was reminded that my existence was an inconvenience; always too loud for some, and too quiet for others, never existing how I was expected to. Often, I wondered if disappearing would finally bring them peace. If taking up no space in their world would be the one thing I could finally do right for them. Not because I wanted to, but because I was tired of always being so wrong. This is the pain of a voluntary orphan. A pain that has followed me all my life.

Against All Odds

He loved her against expectation, against tradition, against friendship, against approval, against self-preservation, and against every opposition and disapproval that he met. He loved her against **all** odds.

Lifeless

Once water, now ice
Freezing out every parched beast.
No longer people-pleasing
No longer allowing them to drink from
the generous fountain of her heart.
Lifeless, cold
No longer a spring of hope;
They've used up her quenching kindness
Leaving a barren, faint semblance of who she once was
Fating her to never be the same.

Freedom

It took her two years
Seven months
Four days
And three attempts to leave him.

She hid money
New passports
And airline tickets to escape.

She sold pieces of her soul to save her children
To give them a fighting chance.

Once out
Once they were comfortably far away
For the first time in a long time
She finally felt free.

Her Muse

He is her muse;
A divine being of beauty, inspiration, and safety for her
heart to unravel.
Unbeknownst to him, his very existence gives her the will
to fight,
To keep living,
And the courage to bare her untold stories in the hope they
will inspire or save another.

Reverie

It was just him and I,
His eyes intently watched me as I studied him,
leaning in, pressing my back against the concrete wall.
His fingers gently tangled into my hair, and then—
fireworks.
His lips heated against mine in a deep, sensual kiss that felt
like he had waited lifetimes to kiss me again.

Honey Child

My love, you were dreamt into existence. You were no longer just a happy possibility—you were now my reality. I created you, my body cradling you, ever so gently, nurturing your delicate life into being. I was infatuated, all consumed, blissfully thanking my lucky stars. Your existence gave me new hope; a purpose I knew I was made for. Everything was falling into place—finally. But, as quickly as you blessed my life, you were just as swiftly taken away. The pain so soul-shattering there are no words profound enough to describe its harrowing magnitude. I howled painfully into the night sky for our creator to take away anything else, to take every prized possession I owned, but to please let me keep my baby. Oh, the way I would have given anything to keep you with me. That night, a piece of my soul died with you. And all I can do now is find solace in knowing you will forever be the most loved and cherished thing I almost had, my honey child.

The Art of Love

He came into her life like a hurricane; awakening parts of her soul she never knew existed. Under his fervent gaze, she felt a lifetime of transcendence—a sense of fulfilment as her heart finally found its missing puzzle piece.

The way his eyes fell upon her made her entire being ache for him. She compared their love to that of Romeo and Juliet, or Edward and Bella: that once in an existence type of love. Her heart yearned for him every moment he was away from her. Until one day, he never returned.

Despite her anger and sense of betrayal, she found herself pleading through broken sobs for him to come back to her, even if to only share one more moment in his arms. The minutes turned to hours, the hours into days—the time passing while she stayed frozen in time—this broken shell of a woman she vowed never to be. Her angry heart interpreting the abandonment as an unfair injustice.

She was left with a broken heart and too many unanswered questions, fuelling her hostility while simultaneously igniting her need to write, to purge her pain. Suddenly, the love once had but now lost became her muse. It became her so completely that she could only put pen to paper while channelling her pain.

Just as she had predicted, part of her died as a result of loving him. She spent her life bleeding her heart across the page that was her canvas, baring every scar, hoping her words would heal at least one person from the torment her heart had endured. This was the art of love.

Blossom

Beam like the sun, and everyone around you will blossom.

Her Magic

She was this stunning beam of light,
Lighting up every room she walked into, most times
without even knowing it.
She was magnetic; people adored her, and animals and
children were completely drawn to her.
She was many things to many people, but to him, she was
nothing less than magic.

Fearless

Evoke the fire within you. Allow the urge to ignite consume you. Embrace it all. Let it manifest and grow beyond even what you thought was possible. Feed the flames until they radiate with such intensity they not only become you, but through wildness, you can no longer decipher where you begin, and they end. Feel their fervency soar into the core of your being until you're scintillating, a fiery star.

This is your moment. Allow yourself to not only be fearless but be fearless in the pursuit of what sets your soul on fire.

Taboo

He was my favourite feeling, even despite him being my biggest lie.

Balance

In this dance of life, you have to take what you want. Nobody else can achieve your goals for you. It's time to navigate that delicate tightrope suspended between your dreams and responsibilities. It's that perpetual act of juggling your priorities, passions, and the ever-changing landscape of expectations. You must harmoniously balance your ambitions and self-care, reaching for the stars whilst being grounded in reality. Allow yourself to lightly sway with the winds of fear and doubt—always maintaining your equilibrium—aiming for peace and fulfilment. Declutter your mind and let go of the noise and weight that holds you back from reaching your true potential. Embrace the sense of liberation. Allow yourself to live a lighter and more buoyant existence where your soul dances freely to the song of the possibilities abound.

Him

It is in the arc of his laughter I find solace—a melody that dances through the fibres of my soul, awakening dormant echoes of joy.

His eyes, twin constellations, hold stories untold, each glance a universe of mysteries begging to be explored.

It is within the maze of his mind I wander, captivated by the intricate paths of thought, finding comfort in the depths of his intellect.

His hands, gentle and steady, trace the contours of my existence, leaving traces of a warmth that lingers long after his touch has faded.

But it is in the quiet moments, the spaces between words, where his essence whispers secrets only my heart can hear.

In his flaws, I have discovered perfection—a mosaic of imperfections that form the masterpiece of his being.

And though time may wear away at the edge of my memory, the imprint of his existence will always remain etched upon my soul—a testament to a love that transcends the boundaries of time and space.

Love is...

Love is the uncontrollable surge of butterflies in your stomach, and the seldom raw moments of utter loneliness in between the euphoric all at once.

Trapped

He was a maze she could not escape—nor did she want to.

A Mother's First-born

I am learning to let him go
so he may live the life
I sacrificed in order to
give him the life I never had.

Her Refuge

Writing is her escape,
Poetry, a refuge, a familiar safe haven.
Medicine against the chaos within,
Unmuting her eight-year-old voice.
Gifting her the courage to speak aloud,
To have her pain heard and felt unequivocally.

Bleeding Heart

Despite the heartbreak this man has inflicted upon my
heart,
I cannot bring myself to deny the love once shared between
us.

I cannot deny the moments we shared intertwined,
Cradling one another in hurt and happiness.

I cannot deny that I still have so much love for this man,
That despite every unrelenting sting of pain I am forced to
feel,
My altruistic heart cares more for his healing than that of
my own.

That even in my life's greatest sorrow,
I have found peace in not denying him my love.

Oh, bleeding heart,
Bleeding heart of mine.

Her Infinite Light

She was his lifeline
Their spirits two-halves of the same soul energy
He existed simply because she lived
But if the world were to cease today
And she survived by chance
He would continue to live, to exist through her light.

But if there was suddenly no tomorrow
And she was taken from him
The world would wither, uninhabitable
A dark, forsaken, and lifeless plane
He could no longer endure.

Inspired to Survive

It was during those hard nights when sleep evaded me,
I began writing in a journal.
I secretly wrote of my dreams,
My wishes and aspirations for my future—
anything to transport my mind from my painful reality.
And on the really hard nights,
I would read the entries back to myself,
Allowing the comforting possibility of their
fruition to envelope my heart.
My spirit calmed in relief
as for just one sacred moment,
I felt inspired to survive.

Serenity

With the gemstone moon, a flourishing flower garden,
freedom to write, and the intoxicating scent of coffee,
who couldn't find serenity in this life?

Inescapable

I am consumed by his smile, and the way his hair falls into his eyes. I am fascinated by the way he works with his hands and everything he touches. I envy the clothes hugging his chest, and the ground he walks on. I am lost in each of his different looks, the music of every laugh harmonising through his body. And the one thing I am most certain of is that:

He is the gravity I cannot defy.

Shedding Seasons

As summer inevitably collapses
giving way to the biting cold
Flowers release their petals

Fly away
Shorter days
Longer nights

Loose leaves fluttering in the arctic breeze
The beauty of letting go, a fluted song
articulated by nature's necessity of shedding seasons

In order to become whole once more.

Love Language

It is so hard to put into words the way I feel about you because I love you in ways I have never loved anyone else, but I've decided I at least owe it to you to try:

In you, my heart has found a new language, one created only for you and I; it cannot be spoken aloud but is felt in every glance, every touch, and every moment we share. With you, love feels less like a choice and more like an ocean current that I have been swept into—effortless, natural, and overwhelming in its beauty. You have unlocked parts of my soul I didn't know existed, and now, in your presence, I feel complete in a way I never thought possible. Loving you, my darling, is like breathing; instinctive and essential to my very existence, and yet I find myself wanting you to take my breath away every time you are near.

Beautiful

I wanted what every young girl wanted: for someone beautiful to find me beautiful. I didn't want to hear the words from well-meaning relatives or be complimented by those who spoke out of obligation. I craved the gaze of someone who saw me not just through the lens of my youth but in a way that made me feel extraordinary. I believed that if someone truly beautiful recognised my beauty, it would somehow validate my existence, as though my worth was intrinsically tied to the reflection of admiration in another's eyes.

But as I grew older, I soon learned that this yearning wasn't just about appearances—it was about being seen, truly seen. Beneath the desire to be found beautiful was a deeper longing for acceptance, love, and belonging. I wanted someone who could look past my surface and still find something stunning, something worth holding onto.

In the end, it isn't about finding beauty in someone else, or even them finding it in you—it is about learning to see beauty within yourself.

Alchemic Catalyst

Words are the alchemic catalyst of life;

Transforming

Pain to healing

Tears to smiles

The lost to found

Turning life into something profound.

Stronger

She bears the weight of pain just as the earth endures any
turbulent storm,
a girl fragile yet fierce, shaped by inflicted damage,
devastation she did not incite.

Through each silent battle, she begins to bloom—
unyielding, rising from the dark,
a woman sculpted by struggle, now standing proudly
knowing her worth like the
ocean knows its depths.

Her gentleness, like the mist that softens wild hills, is no
frail thing, but the quiet, untamed strength of a woman who
has weathered every storm and emerged stronger.

War-torn Heart

Beneath our stunning and boundless sky, where the wind roams seemingly so care-free, my heart trembles—not for me, but for all the souls scattered across this war-torn earth. I cannot help but love them all—the quiet faces, the dreaming eyes, the hands that build and break, that cradle and destroy. For in each, I see a flicker of something shared: a whisper of some ancient kinship, as though we are all but fragments of a shared being, bound by an ancient, unspoken design.

Yet how bitter it is, how cruel, to watch how the world is being torn apart. Oh, the agony of distant lands, where brothers rise against brothers, where the rivers run blood red, and the soil swallows the weight of uncomprehensible grief. My heart aches for the sorrow of their bloodshed, for the cries lost within the winds that carry nothing but ash and heartbreak.

How is it that we, who share the same earth, are able to mindlessly strike one another with such hate? How can the stars above shine on fields of ruin, their light falling upon broken homes and shattered dreams?

I long for the day when peace will fall over us like a soft rain upon this weary land, cleansing it of its pain. Until then, my love stretches like the night, aching, yearning— for every soul who suffers, for every heart that beats beneath our war-torn sky.

In every face, I see a brother, a sister, a beloved relative. And so, my heart, though hopeful, is forever bruised, forever torn, as it loves even those who continually choose to wage war, irrevocably wounding the soul of humanity.

Little Girl

It took me far to long
To be kind to myself
To release the guilt
The judgement and shame
That I carried within my soul
But now I see
That little girl
Made to grow up far too soon
Without the love and protection
All children should have
A birth right, not a privilege
Now I gift that little girl
All the love, understanding, and protection she deserved
And watch with pride
As we heal together.

Stilled Wanderlust

I wandered the balmy island streets,
Oceans away from where I'm from.
Thousands of faces I'd love to know,
I effortlessly weaved through the coconut trees,
Earthy,
Wholesomely grounded.
Familiar,
My heart still, yet compounded.
Not a reverie but a place I've always known.
My freedom journey,
Here, I'm whole,
Here, I'm home.

Ex-girlfriend

I hold no claim upon your heart,
Nor dream I ever shall.
Seeing you with another, a roaring jealousy swells,
For what right have I to harbour such a vicious wrath?

You owe me not a single burden of care,
And yet, in silence, I feel the weight of your absence,
When the hours pass unmarked by your voice,
A disappointment I should not cradle.

What I feel in my heart for you I dare not let it breathe,
So when you linger near, I wear a mask,
For though I know the boundaries of this affection,
It matters not—the ache within remains,
A truth I try to conceal, yet cannot hide, nor contain.

Hypocrite's Masquerade

I hate this game of silence, this aching gap between him and I. I don't want this, I swear, yet here I stand, watching him from a distance, pretending not to care. Though every glance at him pulls me in deeper, there's something maddeningly sweet about his absence. A morbid allure wrapped in the pain. To ignore him feels wrong, but I must not refrain. Because loving him means accepting the impossible.

Every time we cross paths, I put on a front. Laughing it off like he doesn't matter, though inside, my heart races with unspoken words. Caught between wanting and letting go. His presence ignites a fierce fire I cannot extinguish. A longing desire wrapped in layers of frustration. So, I play this part, hiding in plain sight, while secretly wishing for a moment of truth that could shatter our silence and reveal what's hidden beneath this hypocrite's masquerade.

Broken Promises

He was a man of few words, but a poet who made promises spun from silver, wrapping them around my heart like a gossamer thread. He knew just what to say, always at the right moment, as if he could read the bruises on my soul and whisper healing. He painted our future with broad strokes, full of bright colours and endless skies, and I believed him. Every. Time.

"I'll never leave you," he'd say, and I let those words settle deep within me, like roots settling into the earth. "You're the only one," he vowed, and I let that become my truth, allowing myself to fall into his promises as if they were a safe harbour from the storms of doubt.

But promises, I learned, can shatter as easily as glass, leaving behind sharp edges that cut deeper than silence. He would break my heart in whispers; the same way he once mended it. Slowly, quietly, until the words I once held close became hollow, echoes of a love I no longer recognised.

I stayed through the lies, through the betrayals that came cloaked in sweet apologies. Every time he tore me apart, he built me back up again with those same words—words that once held meaning, now only serving to keep me tethered to the pain. My trust fell like crumbling walls, piece by piece, until I was left with nothing but the ashes of everything I had once believed in.

And yet, somehow, I couldn't leave. I held on to the hope that love might return, that maybe this time, his actions would match his words. But in the end, it was faith that love could survive the breaking, faith that the man I loved was the man he promised he'd be.

He taught me the difference between empty words and truth, between hope and illusion. Now, I carry the weight of promises never kept, learning to trust the silence where once his voice lingered. And though my heart is shattered, I'm finally beginning to see the strength in walking away from a man who never deserved me at all.

Familiar Stranger

There's a warmth I've never felt, yet it wraps around my heart. A connection undefined, though we've always been apart. There's a voice I've never heard, but it echoes in my soul. A presence I've been waiting for, to make me finally whole. I wonder how it is I yearn for a love that's still a dream—how I can miss the gentle touch of someone so unseen.

Heart Rise

You'll find him where my heart does rise.
And where it sinks beneath the shadowed skies.
In all my peaks and all my plains,
Wandering softly through my veins.
He's the most magical being in my sight,
Stirring my soul with divinely sacred light.

Chains of Love

You pass so lightly through this world, untouched by its
divide,
While I, forever torn, must bear the breach inside.
I mourn the self that lived before,
Unburdened by your name,
Who wandered free, and never knew
The chains of your love and flame.

Unspoken Goodbye

Like time held still, a wound unhealed—
You and I remain.
No parting words, no soft farewell,
Just silence in our wake.
And through the years, the question lingers:
Why was it left undone?
For all my days, I'll seek in vain
The answer never won.

His Spell

She struggles to find a solution to unloving him, unfeeling what he made her feel. Would pouring her soul onto paper help remove the pain? Or should she confront him, exposing the sorrow he cast upon her soul? If she wished deeply upon a star, could she will the feelings away? Now that she has known his love, how can she cast it aside? Each memory a whisper in her mind, like shadows dancing across the walls. His ghost haunts her waking hours, explicitly against her will. Her tears, she gathers, a river they form. To drown the memories that flood her soul and quell the raging storm. But still, her heart, with stubborn grace, will cherish what it feels. And in its depth, the pain remains, a wound that never heals.
Oh, wise winds of fate. Can hearts forget the past? Or must they bear the weight of love, unyielding to the last? In silence, she shall linger, and in shadows she will dwell. For what he took she cannot shed—her heart remains under his spell.

Sweet Surrender

In loving something greater than myself, there dwells an extraordinary anguish—a sweet surrender. It is like the silent despair of an angel, her wings heavy with the burden of unspoken prayers, or the calloused hands of an artist whose brush, though weary, still strives to capture the beauty it cannot fully grasp. With every measured step I take, every inch I get away from you, I feel the ache of all that is forsaken yet dare not to retrace my path.

SOS

Beaten down instead of being raised.
Left to search for love in unsavoury places.
Lived in an array of houses,
Though, never having a home to set down roots.
Surrounded by countless people claiming to be family,
Ever alone in a room full of familiar strangers.
Expected and forced to grow up too soon.
Losing my human right to a childhood.
Taking on parental responsibilities as a child,
Children raising children to merely attempt to survive.
I am, we are, the children who are in a constant state of
survival…
We survive despite our broken hearts and no parents to
catch us when it all becomes too much.

Stranded Heart

Oh, darling, all that we once cherished
Now drifts in sorrowed song—
The words I once dared speak to thee
Are cast like wreckage, long.

Promises, pale and hollow
Lie scattered on the shore
Each vow, a fading shadow
Each hope, forevermore.

And though I yearned to linger
Clasped tight in memory's keep
My heart, that once burned so brightly
In silence, learned to sleep.

Hidden Truths

So swiftly he was to wield scorn as though it were his shield, casting flames with words that stung like the brisk winter wind. He mocked her tender inclinations, scoffed at her whims and dreams, and in each slight, his voice rang cold and sharp.

Yet beneath his mask of bitter derision, his heart pulsed with a fierce, untamed longing. For in each cruel jibe lay the unspoken truth—the fire of desire he could neither confess nor quell, hidden beneath the guise of disdain.

Daydreamer

Everywhere I cast my gaze, I find traces of him. Every melody hums his name, each verse trembles with his presence. I surrender to the tune, adrift in reverie, clinging to the ghostly distant shadows of him, lost in a waking dream where he is summoned by thin air.

Cosmic Forces

One day, cosmic forces will collide, causing the stars to align in such a divine way that the universe will bare all its glory and otherworldly secrets just to prove to you what is possible if you put your everything into something and have faith.

A New Me

I have paid my dues
I have repented for my sins
I have shed layer upon layer of my delicate skin

I have walked away
I have relinquished the past with all my might
I have departed the shadows into the healing light

I am now naked
I am now free
I am now a new version of who I used to be

Sweetest Dreams

You came to me in my dreams again last night, and as always it felt increasingly more vivid. Your earthy scent surrounded me, captivating all my senses—the sound of your voice, more comforting than I should probably admit—and the taste of your kiss still lingering upon my lips. I'm struggling to separate this fantasy from reality— you consume me and undo me so beautifully—my waking nightmare, my dream world bliss.

Measured Lust

The distance between you and I is measured by how much I long to kiss you.

Upon a Star

All I want is to reminisce tonight, but I don't want to think of you. I want to watch the shooting stars, but my mind keeps wondering if you're watching them too.

Shine

With or without your presence in my life, I will live for my own happiness and purpose just as the moon does not need the approval of the sun to shine in her own right.

Amorist

I miss you in every way despite not
having ever met you.

Sensations

I cannot keep lying to myself… I often think about what it would feel like to sleep next to you; to feel you leaning into me, our bodies entangled in an intoxicating cocktail of intimacy, vulnerability, and safety. I imagine your touch is unlike anything I have ever felt before, harmonising as we make love to one another—me watching you watch me unravelling beneath you—revelling in the sensations coursing through my body, mind, and soul.

Meet Me

Darling, meet me in that in-between place, where time bends just enough for us to fit inside it. Where my day begins with you—the sound of your voice—and your night finds its final breath in the warmth of mine. I want to live there with you—between your sunrise and my dusk—where the world is quiet and our hearts speak louder than time ticking on a clock. In that place, there's no distance, no hours to count, only the steady hum of you and me, meeting over and over again in the same eternal moment.

Heaven Sent

One day, you will meet someone, seemingly by chance, unknowingly by destiny.

This person will embody everything in another human-being that you have prayed for, their essence everything you need. You will, for some unfathomable reason, experience an unimaginable connection with this person, a connection that will defy all logic and reason.

There is no mistake. This person has been heaven sent. The universe has conspired with the stars, orchestrating this divine union, guiding this person into your orbit, to guide you, protect you. They have lessons to teach you that are essential to your soul's evolution.

Surrender and trust in this person and their presence. Know that although your shared connection is strong and real, and your love for this person knows no bounds, their time with you on this earth is only temporary—our creator always calls his angels home once their purpose has been fulfilled.

Peaceful

Peaceful.
Exquisitely peaceful.
Like being on the cusp of being asleep and awake.
Brimming the edge of the dream world and consciousness.
That is the peace I feel in your arms.

Acceptance

As with every other broken moment in this life, I find myself writing to you now as we are facing uncertain and worrying times. In my moments of affliction, it is you who always comes to the forefront of my mind. It is only you who seemingly knows the unfeigned depths of my soul and can soothe any qualm that may arise.

I suppose it is because you and I were bound by loss and grief. We understood one another's pain. In hindsight, that was probably the cause of our destruction. What remains unchanged, is how I need you tonight. For you are the one person who accepts me for who I truly am.

Ancestral Love

Pick yourself up and dust yourself off. It is time to swallow your pride and try again. Nobody said it would be easy, but I promise you it will be worth it. You are not alone in this journey you face; you have generations of your ancestor's blood flowing through your veins—harness their strength. Work hard to manifest your dreams and achieve your goals because you are believed in by many, but the real secret is to first believe in yourself.

A Mother's Love

I used to think love had limits—that I could not love
another being more than I loved myself. Then I had
children, and I learned I was wrong. Never in my life have I
loved another so fiercely, nor found my love grows more
with every pastel sunrise and every sun-kissed sunset.

Wombanhood

As women, our given names become secondary at the time
of our first child's birth, for with the blessing of the
existence of the child who makes us a mother, comes the
gift of being called "Mum."

Close to You

For the longest time
All my being craved
Was to be close to you
To reach out and lightly graze my lips
Over the fervent warmth of your golden skin
But now that I have discovered what it means
To be close to another so intimately
I am certain being close to you was never about intimacy
But rather a fear of being alone.

Armour of Gold

A hush between heartbeats,
When the world feels too wild and cold,
Gather the broken pieces of silence,
Wear them like an armour of gold.

Storms bend the strongest tress,
Tears carve the bravest face,
Still we rise, soft yet certain—
Survival its own kind of grace.

Each scar proof of our story,
Each breath a defiant light—
We are not what once broke us,
We are the ones who choose to fight.

Frayed Wings

An angel
And her broken wings
Grounded
Unable to fly away

A purpose
Once held tightly
Lost
In a haze of confusion

Her softness
And her light dulled
Now only
A fragile illusion

Loving you
Unravels her very soul
Yet still
She clings to the ache of you